The Breathing Field

The Breathing Field

MEDITATIONS ON YOGA

Poems by Wyatt Townley

Images by Eric Dinyer

A Bulfinch Press Book
Little, Brown and Company
Boston New York London

For Roderick and Grace -W.T.

For my Mother and Father -E.D.

Design by Courtney Sullivan

First edition

ISBN 0-8212-2794-7

LCCN 2001096449

Bulfinch Press is an imprint and trademark of Little, Brown and Company (Inc.).

Printed in Hong Kong

Let the body drink its deepest breath,
the lower back spread like a constellation
with one lone star swerving.

CONTENTS

REFACE

Remove shoes before entering.

To open this book is to enter a suddenly quiet space. Yoga is being practiced in these pages, a fusion of word and art. This is not a book about poses, but about the yogic experience translated into verbal and visual realms. Such a translation taps the ability of yoga to heal and transform.

The Breathing Field is a companion book for the yoga practitioner as well as the spiritually adventuresome. Initially we may feel we're in the dark, but even in the first poem we're handed a key. Using evocative metaphors and images as guides, we find that the key opens a door that leads to a path. The farther we go along the path, the closer we come to the sanctuary within ourselves.

The path is not always smooth. It leads through a disruption of the familiar toward a release of the past in order to get to where we have been all along: right here, right now.

To undertake this journey, we need to be willing to accept uncertainty and ambiguity, for we are moving from the known into the unknown. This is the great undoing in Part I, using yogic imagery to loosen the body's armor in preparation for moving from outer to inner. Part II takes us inward, crossing mental and physical boundaries that we've spent a lifetime fortifying. The last section breaks through to life beyond the body, where the self expands and healing begins.

Healing is integration. Our mission is to marry the parts of us that have become disjointed: left brain and right brain, mind and body, word and image. This is the way of yoga, which means "yoking together." It is also the way of a certain kind of breath-based, spirit-based poetry when joined to a deep-reaching visual art.

In the past, artists and poets have tended to operate in separate worlds. That makes sense, since visual images are perceived all at once, while the eye must piece together words in a linear sequence. In fact, the two arts appear to involve different areas of the brain. "Written words and images are entirely different 'creatures,'" writes cultural anthropologist Leonard Shlain. "Each calls forth a complementary but opposing perceptual strategy."

In *The Breathing Field,* these creatures have fused, giving birth to an artistic life-form like no other. It is a form with the life-breath in it. Breath is the path that unrolls through these pages—and is the book's central metaphor. It is the path that yogis travel, connecting the upper and lower body, heart and pelvis. It is the path that winds through the paintings of Fauvist artist Maurice Vlaminck. It is Robert Frost's road less traveled and Walt Whitman's "Song of the Open Road."

You are already on it. Inhale and turn the page.

Part I

Undoing

THE KEY

Here, inside the chest
a tiny fear is folded
neatly like a sweater

in the top drawer.
Take it out. Shake it.
Have a look. Open

the middle drawer.
The cries of a child
stab through you

until her sobs are yours.
In the bottom drawer
under a stack of gowns

is a clenched fist.
It is holding *clink!* a key
that falls at your feet.

CORPSE POSE

At the end of your mat at the edge
of the beanfield, the orchard rises,
tree after tree, a door behind a door

behind the years that fling themselves
into orbit, running rings around
each other, counting the way back

to center. We count back ourselves,
behind the children we've spun off,
houses we built, clothes we've shed,

flesh, muscle, bone, to the river that
underlies us, solid and fluid, trunk
and sap, vertebra and cord. Close

the eyes and lean into the current.
Slide under the scars where meteors dug
their graves in us millennia ago. Count

back, count sheep, count your blessings,
count your silver as your mother first
counted your toes, go back before the

numbers that put us in our places
where we have held firm ever since,
row on row, to the end of the beanfield,

at the edge of your mat where you are
still lying, with everything you ever had,
to see if this breath is your last.

THE SWING

A line branches out
between your eyebrows.
It is the tree of cares.

Climb it and look down.
From here everything looks
smaller. This is the place

where you fall in the dream
where the tiger enters
where the curtain goes up

and you have on no clothes.
Look. There, behind the
actor, the tiger, the crack

in the drive, another appears
on cue. Behind the last fear
is an empty swing.

SWIMMING LESSON

Go under.
Put your whole head in
like the potato that grows
below the feet, below
concrete and the cars
that carry us.

We get up and dress up
and build up and grow
up. The potato grows down.
It underlies everything
we have made
or said, or haven't.

The potato shows us
where we are
heading. Dive in. Put
your whole life
into it.

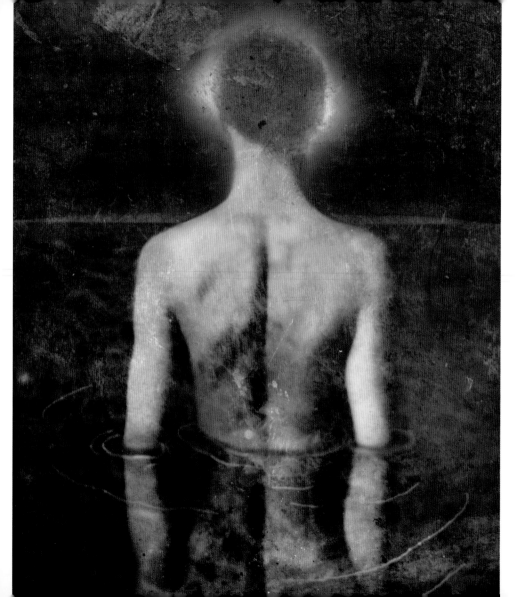

THE FIRE TAKES SHAPE

This fistful of stars
strewn across darkness

burned out long ago
in the shape of your initials

and what is to come
is quite out of our

hands. Let go. We
are galaxies in a head-on

collusion millions
of years ago

before we dreamed
ourselves here. Everything

we see is past. Witness
Cassiopeia. Just last month she

rose from her chair. Orion,
poised to shoot, has set

down his bow and crossed
over. *Et tu?* Listen:

behind the ringing
ears and the waterfall

of breath is a burning so seductive
you cannot turn away.

THE STORM IN THE BODY

We've seen it coming, the one
that is the end of us.
We've heard it reversing

the corn's perfect aisles,
roaring through what it takes
to get home, bull's-eye, trash

it rummaged through whole
worlds to find. For years
we've felt a trembling in the teacups,

and now it's a straight line
through cedars to the torn
flags of our lids *as the storm at last enters, unsnaps the jaw, tunnels*

        the throat, yanks out the scream

           to touch down

             in the dark

              dark

             cave

             of

             the

              belly

             where

             we

            come

             a-

part   *like the walls*

             of the house we

grew   *up in*

Part II

Stepping Over

WHAT KEEPS US STILL

The wind began you,
your father's sighs
threading my own

and then the wind birthed
you, the long, slow
knife of exhalation.

It was wind that sirened
out the tunnel
of your first cry

and now wind streams
through your coatsleeves
to the distant arms

of Three Oaks. It's
what lifts the fringe
of hair on the nape

then flattens a house
ten miles away,
returning

to the deepest
well of the womb
where we begin

our second birth,
breath by quiet
breath. Wind's

what tends the fire
that will burn
beyond us all.

LEAVE OF ABSENCE

After all, we are water
                    seeking our lowest
level at high tide. Lie

                    down and let waves roll
behind the brow. Schools
                    swim from the corners

of eyes, under upturned
                    rocks. The eyebrows drift,
silver canoes, to unseen

                    horizons. Drop the jaw,
bobbing in its slip. Uncoil
                    the rope in the lips.

Inhale. Sail the undertow
                    from atlas to coccyx.
We are Magellan,

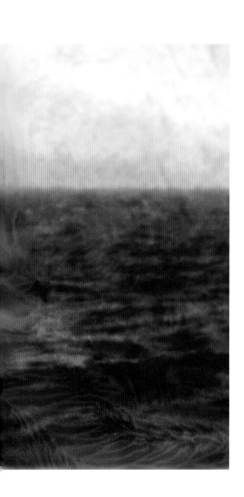

heading to the bottom
of the New World,
its curling tip beckoning

off the end of the map.
Here is the glimpsed
place we remember

forgetting. Open your
hands and keep going,
steering with the eyes

closed. "My goal is to
disappear," said the yogi.
Exhale. Feel the front

rush into the back
that falls into the earth
that plunges into space.

41

HAVING SPINE

I

A string of shells on the ocean floor
that mother and grandmother grew

in the dark, pushed from the depth
of the belly, wave by wave, into

a hardening world. The spine twists
behind a lectern. Tucks into a chair

in the back row. Shoved
against a lover, thirty-three stones

skip across a lake, looking for home.

2

Having spine tells us from them.
Keeps us from snaking around.

It's pure chameleon: water, fire,
earth, air. Feel it turn

into mermaid, hot-air balloon,
flight of stairs, waterspout. . . .

French windows swing
over the bay. The moon

streams in. A cat jumps out.

3

When it hurts, crawl like the sea
turtle to where you began.

Feel the tide turn back to shore.
Ride it in. Let the moon

pull through you. Now it's time
for stillness, pillows and ice.

Breathe through the lace
curtains of your back.

Fall into place. And falling, rise.

4

Breathing takes a lifetime,
downshifting from chest to belly.

We exhale for miles, fanning the fire
from window to window. Buildings

fall in a breath. This is the path
of no shortcut, the way of light

between then and now. The wind
licks your spine. Let the flames rise

up, burning you down.

5

Toss a bone into water.
Concentric circles move

to every shore. A wave laps
against the back of a swimmer

in the distance. In the lamplight
someone is rocking, head bowed

to a book. The spine curves
over the poem like a question,

fills with nerve and takes flight.

THE SACRED BONE

ignites on contact   at this holy crossing
with a touching of wires   where spire meets horizon
a fusion of bone   andspinebecomespelvis
throwing off sparks   the sun roars through you
kindled by wind into fire   gold   orange   blue

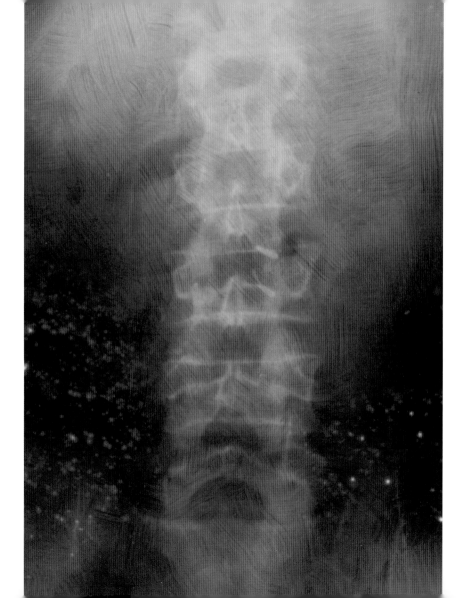

BLUE TELESCOPE

Follow the wind that feeds the fire
that follows the spine that spreads beyond
what formerly was you, the low back
smearing into sunset as stars slip into place

your eyes beam out across the coming
night through a yellow window whose
curtains rise with wind that moves a page
across a desk on which a name is scrawled

in the hand that stroked the throat
of a long-haired cat who purred all day
on a velvet couch as bellies of leaves
shimmered from tree to tree in which catbirds

were growing in small green eggs, watched
by a curious child behind a blue telescope

Part III

Reverse Zoom

THE BREATHING FIELD

Between each vertebra
is the through line
of your life's story,
where the setting sun
has burned all colors
into the cord. Step

over. Put on the dark
shirt of stars.
A full moon rises
over the breathing field,
seeps into clover and the brown
lace of its roots
where insects are resting

their legs. Take in the view.
So much is still
to be seen. Get back
behind your back, behind
what is behind you.

HOW TO GET TALL

Inhale what the tree gives
you. Exhale what it needs.

Feel its leaves, sure as hands,
stroke the front of your spine.

Inhale, drinking the wind
deep into the trunk. This

is an art. Breathe out
through cobwebs and vines.

We are getting to a place
where the tree can start

to live on its own. Push
its crown from your core.

Then give birth. Grow
out of everything you were.

HEARD AT STAR CEMETERY

Four walls wrap this place
like a string around a shoebox
in which the earth is kicking.
At night stars throw themselves
onto graves of children and the wind
drives through an alley of cedars.

Here is the plot we've chosen,
where valleys meet hills like the top
of a woman's thighs, this dark seam
light must find its way through.

We weave through gravestones
and cross the fence, looking for milkweed
to settle a wart, when the rain starts.

It's the same refrain that ricochets
from tree to tree across the world:
Someone has died, someone is sobbing.
Whoever said we can't be in two
places at once? We're chords, a plash
of notes thrown together in time.

# ARS POETICA

What's the farthest sound you hear
                    beyond the wall
                                        through the shifting

branches, down the carpet
                    of streets then fields
                                        where clover unrolls

through a tunnel of trees
                    to the bench
                                        where a pen

scratches its small rows
                    from left to right,
                                        left to right?

Meet the farmer

       of ears and eyes.

              You are being cultivated.

The shadow

       of the hand

              grows larger than the hand

pushing its stick

       across a line

              until there is no line to cross,

no hand to squeeze.

       Just you who listens,

              and who sees.

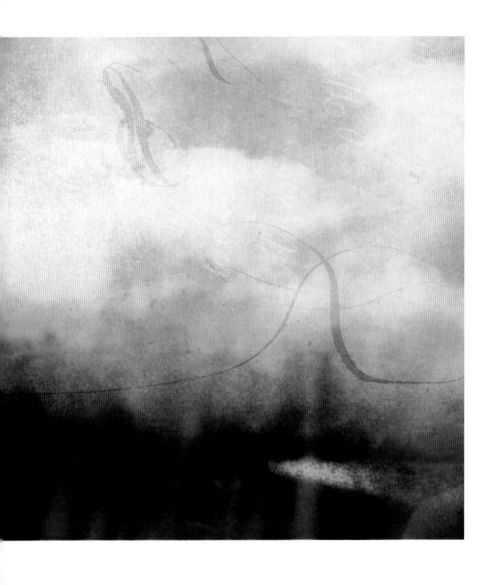

PRAYER FOR A NEW MILLENNIUM

On the first evening
buzzing with the last light
that skids through everything,
let the body drink its deepest
breath, the lower back
spread like a constellation
with one lone star swerving.
Let the hands, lined with meteors,
open, releasing all they have held —
coins, hammers, steering
wheels and the silken
faces of children — to find
what on earth they really hold.
Let the crown of the head
move away from the shoulders
and into the distance
where another is waiting.

Let go of the forecast you heard
when you were younger
than the child now clattering
up the backstairs all
laughter and gasping
for what we're here to do.
Look down. Look at the stars.
We're here so briefly, weather
with bones.

Acknowledgments

Grateful acknowledgment goes to the editors of the following publications where these poems first appeared, often in different form:

Yoga Journal	"The Breathing Field"
Southern Poetry Review	"Prayer for a New Millennium"
Orion	"The Fire Takes Shape"
New Letters	"What Keeps Us Still"
The Midwest Quarterly	"The Storm in the Body"
The Kansas City Star	"Heard at Star Cemetery"

"Having Spine" won a Hackney National Literary Award and the Kansas Voices Poetry Prize.

"Prayer for a New Millennium" also appeared in *Prayers for a Thousand Years,* edited by Elias Amidon and Elizabeth Roberts (HarperSanFrancisco, 1999), and is quoted in *Fruitflesh: Seeds of Inspiration for Women Who Write,* by Gayle Brandeis (HarperSanFrancisco, 2002). "Swimming Lesson" appeared in *Spud Songs,* edited by Gloria Vando and Robert Stewart (Helicon Nine Editions, 1999). "Ars Poetica" appeared in *Poets at Large,* edited by Harvey Hix (Helicon Nine Editions, 1996).

Thanks also to the following for their help along the path: Roderick Townley, Sandy Choron, Dorothy Williams, Helen Watt, Courtney Sullivan, Christine and Ryan Dinyer, Joanne and Russell Baker, Grace Townley, Genevieve Crosslin, Don Dubowski, Dr. Jo Jeanne Callaway, Helen Ravenhill, Carre Bevilacqua, Amy Farr Borgman, Eric Beeler, Harry Smith, past and present students of Yoganetics, and Mildred's coffee house.

About the Author & Artist

The Author

Wyatt Townley's first book, *Perfectly Normal* (New York: The Smith), was a finalist for the Yale Series of Younger Poets, and her poems and essays have been published in magazines ranging from *The Paris Review* to *Yoga Journal* to *Newsweek*. Formerly a dancer, Wyatt is the founder of Yoganetics® (from "yoga" and "kinetic"), a fitness system that extends yoga into motion (www.yoganetics.com). Designer of workouts for national magazines, Wyatt has also produced a video, *Yoganetics: Relaxation & Basic Workout*, and the book *Yoganetics: Fitness from the Inside Out* (forthcoming from HarperSanFrancisco). *The Breathing Field* stems from a lifelong passion to yoke the arts of yoga and poetry into a single expression of spirit.

The Artist

Eric Dinyer is an internationally acclaimed artist/illustrator who has worked in the entertainment, music, and publishing industries for many years. His art has appeared on numerous book covers and in magazines, motion pictures and television. A recipient of the Silver Medal from the Society of Illustrators, Eric created the CD cover of Bruce Springsteen's *The Ghost of Tom Joad* and worked on Sting's interactive CD-ROM, *All This Time*. He received his M.F.A. from the School of Visual Arts in New York and in 1998 joined forces with designer David Decheser to form Dreamless Studios (www.dreamless.com). A dedicated yoga practitioner, he combines in this book his passion for yoga with his lifelong commitment to art.